Table of contents

In a world where shadows often cloud the brightest of souls, "Embracing the Light Within is a heartfelt guide that seeks to illuminate the path of those struggling with depression. This book aims to offer solace, understanding and practical tools to navigate the depths while igniting the spark of hope and resilience to every reader

Depression is a complex mental health condition characterized by persistent feelings of sadness, hopelessness, and a lack of interest in activities. It can affect a person's thoughts, emotions, and physical well-being. Shedding light on depression involves understanding its nature, causes, and dispelling common misconceptions.

Nature of Depression:

- **Multifaceted Condition:** Depression is not a one-size-fits-all condition. It can manifest in various forms, including major depressive disorder, persistent depressive disorder (dysthymia), bipolar disorder, and seasonal affective disorder.
- **Physical and Psychological Impact:** Depression is not solely a psychological issue. It has physical manifestations, such as changes in sleep patterns, appetite, and energy levels. It can also lead to physical symptoms like headaches and digestive problems.
- **Chronic and Recurrent:** Depression can be chronic, lasting for an extended period, or it can be episodic with recurrent episodes throughout a person's life.

Causes of Depression:

- **Biological Factors:** Genetic predisposition, chemical imbalances in the brain (particularly involving neurotransmitters like serotonin), and alterations in brain structure and function can contribute to depression.
- **Environmental Factors:** Adverse life events, trauma, chronic stress, and a lack of social support can play a significant role in triggering or exacerbating depression.
- **Psychological Factors:** Certain personality traits, such as low self-esteem, a tendency toward perfectionism, or a history of other mental health disorders, may contribute to the development of depression.
- **Medical Conditions:** Chronic illnesses, hormonal changes, and certain medications can increase the risk of depression.

Common Misconceptions:

- **It's Just Sadness:** Depression is more than just feeling sad. While sadness is a normal emotion, depression involves persistent and intense feelings of despair, hopelessness, and a lack of interest in activities.
- **Weakness or Laziness:** Depression is not a sign of weakness or laziness. is a medical condition with complex underlying factors, and individuals with depression often face considerable challenges in their daily lives.
- **It Will Just Go Away:** While some individuals may experience temporary periods of low mood, clinical depression usually requires treatment. Ignoring it or hoping it will go away on its own can lead to worsening symptoms and prolonged suffering.

- **It Affects Only Certain Types of People:** Depression can affect anyone, regardless of age, gender, socioeconomic status, or background. It is a widespread and inclusive mental health condition.
- **Medication Alone is Always Sufficient:** While medication can be an essential component of treatment for some individuals, it is often most effective when combined with psychotherapy, lifestyle changes, and support from friends and family.

Understanding depression involves recognizing its complexity and addressing it as a legitimate medical condition. If you or someone you know is experiencing symptoms of depression, it is crucial to seek professional help for an accurate diagnosis and appropriate treatment.

Recognizing the signs and symptoms of depression is crucial for early intervention and effective treatment. Depression can manifest in various ways, and individuals may experience a combination of symptoms. It's important to note that the severity and duration of symptoms can vary. Here are common signs and manifestations of depression:

Emotional Symptoms:

- **Persistent Sadness:** A pervasive feeling of sadness, emptiness, or hopelessness that lasts most of the day, nearly every day.
- **Loss of Interest or Pleasure:** Diminished interest or pleasure in activities that were once enjoyable, including hobbies, socializing, or sex.
- **Irritability:** Increased irritability, frustration, or feelings of being easily annoyed, even over minor matters.
- **Changes in Mood:** Mood swings, ranging from feeling excessively guilty or worthless to experiencing heightened anxiety.

Cognitive Symptoms:

- **Difficulty Concentrating:** Trouble focusing, making decisions, or remembering details.
- **Negative Thoughts:** Persistent negative thoughts about oneself, the future, or the world. These may include thoughts of death or suicide.

Physical Symptoms:

- **Changes in Appetite:** Significant weight loss or gain due to changes in appetite, leading to overeating or loss of interest in food.
- **Sleep Disturbances:** Insomnia (difficulty falling or staying asleep) or hypersomnia (excessive sleeping).
- **Fatigue:** Persistent feelings of fatigue, low energy, and a sense of being physically drained.

Behavioural Symptoms:

- **Social Withdrawal:** Withdrawal from social activities, isolation from friends and family, and a reluctance to engage in usual activities.
- **Neglect of Responsibilities:** Decline in performance at work or school, neglect of responsibilities, and a sense of being overwhelmed.
- **Physical Agitation or Slowed Movements:** Restlessness or slowed physical movements noticeable by others.

Physical Manifestations:

- **Aches and Pains:** Unexplained physical complaints such as headaches, stomach-aches, or muscle pain.

Different Manifestations:

- **Major Depressive Disorder (MDD):** Characterized by persistent and severe symptoms that interfere with daily functioning. MDD often involves recurrent episodes.
- **Persistent Depressive Disorder (Dysthymia):** Involves long-term, chronic symptoms that are less severe than MDD but last for at least two years.
- **Bipolar Disorder (BPD):** Involves episodes of both depression and mania (elevated mood, increased energy, impulsivity). BPD has distinct depressive phases.
- **Seasonal Affective Disorder (SAD):** Depression that occurs seasonally, often in the winter months when there is less sunlight.
- **Psychotic Depression:** Depression accompanied by psychotic symptoms, such as hallucinations or delusions.

Recognizing depression requires paying attention to changes in behaviour, mood, and physical well-being. If you or someone you know is experiencing symptoms of depression, seeking professional help from a mental health provider is crucial. Depression is a treatable condition, and early intervention can make a significant difference in the prognosis and quality of life.

Depression is not only characterized by persistent feelings of sadness but also involves a complex web of emotions that can vary from person to person. Exploring the emotional landscape of depression involves unravelling the intricate tapestry of feelings that individuals may experience. Here are some key emotional aspects commonly associated with depression:

1. Despair and Hopelessness:

- A pervasive sense of despair and hopelessness about the future.
- Feeling trapped in a cycle of negative thoughts with little prospect for improvement.

2. Guilt and Worthlessness:

- Overwhelming feelings of guilt, even for minor mistakes or perceived shortcomings.
- A deep sense of worthlessness and a belief that one is a burden to others.

3. Emotional Numbness:

- Some individuals may experience emotional numbness, a feeling of being detached from their own emotions.
- Difficulty experiencing joy or pleasure, even in activities that were once enjoyable.

4. Anxiety and Fear:

- Heightened anxiety and fear, often accompanied by irrational worries and a sense of impending doom.
- Physical symptoms of anxiety, such as restlessness, tension, and a racing heart.

5. Anger and Irritability:

- Increased irritability and a short temper, often directed towards oneself or others.
- Feelings of anger, frustration, and a sense of being overwhelmed by negative emotions.

6. Loneliness and Isolation:

- Intense feelings of loneliness and isolation, even when surrounded by others.
- Difficulty connecting with friends and family, leading to a sense of social withdrawal.

7. Loss and Grief:

- Grieving for the loss of interest in life, the loss of one's sense of self, or the loss of relationships affected by depression.
- Mourning the loss of a hopeful and positive outlook on life.

8. Shame:

- A deep sense of shame about the condition, leading to reluctance to seek help or share feelings with others.
- Internalized stigma associated with mental health issues.

9. Emotional Exhaustion:

- Overwhelming emotional exhaustion and a constant feeling of being drained.
- The struggle to cope with daily life demands due to the emotional burden of depression.

10. Suicidal Thoughts:

- In some cases, individuals may experience thoughts of death or suicide as a way to escape the emotional pain.

Understanding this emotional landscape is crucial for both individuals experiencing depression and those supporting them. It emphasizes the need for a comprehensive approach to treatment that addresses not only the core symptoms of depression but also the underlying emotional complexities. Professional support, such as therapy and counselling, can provide a safe space to explore and navigate these complex emotions, fostering a path toward healing and recovery.

Self-compassion is a powerful and transformative quality that involves treating oneself with kindness, understanding, and acceptance, especially during times of difficulty or failure. It encompasses being mindful of one's own struggles without judgment and recognizing that suffering is a shared human experience. The power of self-compassion is evident in various aspects of mental, emotional, and physical well-being:

1. Improved Mental Health:

- **Reduced Negative Self-Talk:** Self-compassion helps individuals cultivate a more positive and understanding internal dialogue, reducing harsh self-criticism.
- **Lower Levels of Anxiety and Depression:** Embracing oneself with compassion has been linked to lower levels of anxiety and depression, fostering a more resilient mindset.

2. Emotional Resilience:

- **Coping with Failure:** When faced with setbacks or failures, individuals with self-compassion are more likely to bounce back, learn from the experience, and move forward.
- **Emotional Regulation:** Self-compassion contributes to better emotional regulation by acknowledging and validating emotions without judgment.

3. Increased Motivation:

- **Intrinsic Motivation:** Self-compassionate individuals are often motivated by a desire for personal growth and well-being rather than external validation or fear of failure.
- **Encourages Learning:** Instead of being paralyzed by fear of making mistakes, self-compassion encourages a mindset of curiosity and learning.

4. Enhanced Relationships:

- **Greater Empathy:** Individuals who practice self-compassion are often more empathetic and understanding toward others, fostering healthier interpersonal relationships.
- **Reduced Social Comparison:** By embracing one's own imperfections, there is less inclination to constantly compare oneself to others, leading to more authentic connections.

5. Physical Well-Being:

- **Stress Reduction:** Self-compassion has been associated with lower levels of stress and cortisol, promoting overall physical health.
- **Better Health Choices:** People with self-compassion are more likely to make healthier lifestyle choices, such as exercise and balanced nutrition.

6. Increased Self-Esteem:

- **Stable Self-Worth:** Self-compassion is linked to a more stable and authentic sense of self-worth, less dependent on external validation.
- **Less Perfectionism:** Individuals practicing self-compassion are often less burdened by perfectionism, allowing for a more realistic and positive self-image.

7. Mindfulness and Presence:

- **Present Moment Awareness:** Self-compassion involves being present with one's experiences, fostering mindfulness and reducing rumination about the past or anxiety about the future.
- **Acceptance of Impermanence:** Recognizing that difficult emotions and situations are temporary helps individuals navigate challenges with greater ease.

8. Spiritual Well-Being:

- **Connection to a Higher Purpose:** Some individuals find that self-compassion connects them to a sense of purpose or a higher meaning in life.

Cultivating self-compassion involves practice and self-awareness. Techniques such as self-compassion meditations, journaling, and mindfulness exercises can be effective tools in developing this powerful and transformative quality. As individuals learn to treat themselves with the same kindness and understanding they would offer to a friend, they unlock the potential for resilience, growth, and overall well-being.

Cultivating kindness, acceptance, and forgiveness toward oneself is a transformative process that can significantly contribute to overall well-being and mental health. Here are some strategies to foster these positive qualities:

1. Practice Self-Compassion:

- **Mindful Self-Compassion Meditation:** Engage in mindfulness practices that specifically focus on self-compassion. This involves acknowledging and accepting difficult emotions with kindness.
- **Self-Compassionate Letter:** Write a letter to yourself, expressing understanding and compassion for any challenges you're facing. Treat yourself as you would a dear friend.

2. Develop a Positive Self-Talk:

- **Challenge Negative Thoughts:** Actively challenge and reframe negative self-talk. Replace self-critical thoughts with more balanced and compassionate statements.
- **Use Affirmations:** Create and repeat positive affirmations that emphasize self-love, acceptance, and forgiveness.

3. Mindfulness and Acceptance:

- **Non-Judgmental Awareness:** Practice mindfulness to cultivate non-judgmental awareness of your thoughts and feelings. Accept them without attaching value judgments.
- **Radical Acceptance:** Embrace the concept of radical acceptance, acknowledging and accepting the reality of your current situation without resistance.

4. Forgiveness:

- **Understand Imperfection:** Recognize that being human involves making mistakes and experiencing imperfections. Understand that mistakes do not define your worth.

- **Release Resentment:** Work on letting go of resentment toward yourself for past actions or decisions. Understand that growth often arises from learning experiences.

5. Gratitude Practice:

- **Focus on Positives:** Develop a gratitude practice by regularly reflecting on positive aspects of yourself and your life. This can shift your focus from self-criticism to appreciation.
- **Gratitude Journal:** Keep a journal where you write down things you are grateful for, including positive qualities and achievements.

6. Set Realistic Expectations:

- **Embrace Realism:** Set realistic and achievable goals for yourself. Avoid setting standards that are too high and may lead to self-criticism.
- **Celebrate Progress:** Acknowledge and celebrate even small achievements and progress. Pat yourself on the back for efforts made.

7. Seek Support:

- **Therapy or Counselling:** Consider seeking the support of a mental health professional who can provide guidance and tools for cultivating self-kindness, acceptance, and forgiveness.
- **Connect with Others:** Share your thoughts and feelings with trusted friends or family members who can offer empathy and support.

8. Self-Care Practices:

- **Prioritize Self-Care:** Implement self-care routines that prioritize your physical and emotional well-being. This can include activities you genuinely enjoy and that nourish your soul.
- **Set Boundaries:** Learn to set healthy boundaries to protect your emotional and mental space.

9. Mindful Self-Forgiveness:

- **Acknowledge Growth:** Reflect on your journey and acknowledge the growth and changes you've experienced. Understand that personal evolution is a continuous process.
- **Release Guilt:** Let go of guilt associated with past actions. Understand that mistakes are opportunities for learning and growth.

Cultivating kindness, acceptance, and forgiveness toward oneself is an ongoing process that requires patience and self-compassion. Be gentle with yourself, recognizing that these practices can contribute to a more positive and fulfilling life.

Nurturing self-care practices is a vital aspect of maintaining overall well-being, both physically and mentally. Self-care routines have the power to unveil healing potential and contribute to a more balanced and fulfilling life. Here are some self-care practices and their healing benefits:

1. Physical Self-Care:

- **Regular Exercise:** Engaging in physical activity releases endorphins, reduces stress hormones, and promotes overall physical health.
- **Adequate Sleep:** Prioritize quality sleep, as it plays a crucial role in physical and mental recovery.

2. Emotional Self-Care:

- **Journaling:** Writing down thoughts and feelings can provide a healthy emotional outlet and promote self-reflection.
- **Mindfulness and Meditation:** These practices foster emotional awareness, reduce stress, and improve overall emotional well-being.

3. Social Self-Care:

- **Quality Time with Loved Ones:** Spending time with friends and family can provide emotional support and strengthen social connections.
- **Setting Boundaries:** Learning to set boundaries in relationships contributes to emotional well-being.

4. Intellectual Self-Care:

- **Continuous Learning:** Engaging in activities that stimulate the mind, such as reading, learning a new skill, or pursuing a hobby, enhances cognitive function.
- **Mind-challenging Games:** Playing games or solving puzzles can be intellectually stimulating and enjoyable.

5. Spiritual Self-Care:

- **Meditation and Reflection:** These practices help connect with a sense of purpose, meaning, and spirituality.
- **Nature Connection:** Spending time in nature can promote a sense of awe and spiritual connectedness.

6. Pampering and Relaxation:

- **Hot Baths or Showers:** Warm water can relax muscles and provide a soothing experience.
- **Aromatherapy:** Essential oils and calming scents can positively impact mood and relaxation.

7. Creativity and Expression:

- **Artistic Outlets:** Engaging in creative activities, such as drawing, painting, or writing, allows for self-expression and stress relief.
- **Music and Dance:** Listening to music or dancing can be uplifting and provide an emotional outlet.

8. Digital Detox:

- **Unplugging:** Taking breaks from electronic devices can reduce stress and promote mindfulness.
- **Nature Walks:** Spending time outdoors without digital distractions can have a calming effect.

9. Healthy Nutrition:

- **Balanced Diet:** Consuming a nutritious and balanced diet supports physical health and can positively impact mood.
- **Hydration:** Staying adequately hydrated is essential for overall well-being.

10. Therapeutic Practices:

- **Massage or Bodywork:** Physical touch through massage can reduce muscle tension and promote relaxation.
- **Therapy or Counselling:** Seeking professional support allows for exploration and resolution of emotional challenges.

11. Gratitude Practice:

- **Gratitude Journaling:** Reflecting on positive aspects of life fosters a positive mindset and enhances emotional well-being.
- **Expressing Thanks:** Expressing gratitude to others strengthens social connections and promotes a positive atmosphere.

12. Quality Alone Time:

- **Solitude:** Spending time alone allows for self-reflection and relaxation, fostering a sense of independence and self-awareness.

Self-care practices are not only about pampering oneself but are essential for maintaining balance, preventing burnout, and supporting overall health. Regularly incorporating these practices into daily life can unveil the healing potential of self-care and contribute to a more resilient and fulfilling life.

Rewriting negative self-talk involves transforming critical and unhelpful thoughts into more constructive and supportive statements. This process can contribute to improved self-esteem and a more positive mindset. Here are some examples of how to reframe negative self-talk:

1. **Negative Thought: "I'm always making mistakes."**
   - **Reframed Thought: "I am learning and growing from my experiences. Mistakes are opportunities for improvement, not a reflection of my worth."

2. **Negative Thought: "I'll never be good enough."**
   - **Reframed Thought: "I am constantly evolving and doing my best. I acknowledge my progress and celebrate my efforts."

3. **Negative Thought: "I can't handle this; it's too much for me."**
   - **Reframed Thought: "I may face challenges, but I have the strength and resilience to overcome them. I can take things one step at a time."

4. **Negative Thought: "Nobody likes me; I'm always alone."**
   - **Reframed Thought: "I have people who care about me, and I am worthy of connection. I can take steps to nurture and build relationships."

5. **Negative Thought: "I always mess things up."**
   - **Reframed Thought: "I make mistakes, and that's okay. I can learn from them and apply those lessons to do better next time."

6. **Negative Thought: "I'm a failure."**
   - **Reframed Thought: "I may not succeed at everything, but that doesn't define my worth. Each experience, whether a success or a setback, contributes to my growth."

7. **Negative Thought: "I'll never be as good as others."**
   - **Reframed Thought: "I am unique, and my journey is my own. I can appreciate others' strengths without diminishing my own."

8. **Negative Thought: "I'm too lazy; I'll never accomplish anything."**
   - **Reframed Thought: "I may feel overwhelmed at times, but I have the ability to set realistic goals and take steps toward achieving them. Progress is a process."

9. **Negative Thought: "I'm not smart enough to handle this."**
   - **Reframed Thought: "I have the intelligence and capacity to learn and adapt. I will approach challenges with curiosity and a willingness to grow."

10. **Negative Thought: "I always let people down."**
   - **Reframed Thought: "While I may have disappointed others in the past, I am committed to learning and improving. I can communicate and work towards understanding."

11. **Negative Thought: "I don't deserve happiness."**
  - **Reframed Thought: "I am deserving of happiness and fulfilment. I will actively seek and create moments of joy in my life."

12. **Negative Thought: "I'll never get it right."**
  - **Reframed Thought: "It's okay not to be perfect. I will approach challenges with patience, and each attempt is an opportunity for progress."

Remember that changing negative self-talk takes time and practice. Consistently challenging and reframing these thoughts can contribute to a more positive and compassionate inner dialogue.

Challenging and transforming self-defeating thoughts involves developing awareness, questioning negative beliefs, and replacing them with more positive and constructive perspectives. Here are techniques to help you challenge and transform self-defeating thoughts:

Consistency is key when implementing these techniques. Experiment with different strategies to find what works best for you and remember that transforming self-defeating thoughts is a gradual process that involves practice and self-compassion.

Challenging and transforming self-defeating thoughts involves developing awareness, questioning negative beliefs, and replacing them with more positive and constructive perspectives. Here are techniques to help you challenge and transform self-defeating thoughts:

. Mindfulness and Awareness:

- **Mindful Observation:** Notice when negative thoughts arise without judgment. Simply observe them without immediately accepting them as true.
- **Mindfulness Meditation:** Practice mindfulness meditation to cultivate awareness of your thoughts and emotions.

. Cognitive Restructuring:

- **Identify Negative Thoughts:** Pay attention to negative thoughts and write them down. Identify patterns in your thinking.
- **Question the Evidence:** Challenge the evidence supporting your negative thoughts. Ask yourself if there are alternative interpretations or evidence to the contrary.

3. Thought Records:

- **ABC Model:** Use the ABC model (Activating event, Beliefs, Consequences) to examine situations, identify your beliefs, and explore the emotional consequences.
- **Thought Record Worksheets:** Complete thought record worksheets to analyse and reframe negative thoughts systematically.

4. Reality Testing:

- **Is it a Fact or Interpretation?** Differentiate between facts and interpretations. Question whether your thoughts are based on objective facts or personal interpretations.
- **Consult Others:** Seek feedback from trusted friends or family to gain different perspectives on situations.

5. Positive Affirmations:

- **Create Positive Statements:** Develop positive affirmations that counteract negative beliefs. Repeat them regularly to reinforce a more positive mindset.
- **Visualizations:** Combine positive affirmations with visualization technique to create a mental image of success and positivity.

6. Behavioural Experiments:

- **Test Negative Assumptions:** Conduct small experiments to test the validity of negative assumptions. Experiencing success in these experiments can challenge and transform negative beliefs.
- **Behavioural Activation:** Engage in activities that bring a sense of accomplishment and pleasure, challenging thoughts that suggest you're incapable or unworthy.

7. Gratitude Practice:

- **Focus on the Positive:** Cultivate a gratitude practice to shift your focus from what's wrong to what's going well in your life.
- **Gratitude Journal:** Regularly write down things you are grateful for to reinforce positive thinking.

8. Self-Compassion Techniques:

- **Self-Compassionate Letter:** Write a letter to yourself with kindness and understanding, emphasizing self-compassion.
- **Mindful Self-Compassion:** Practice mindful self-compassion exercises to develop a more nurturing and supportive inner dialogue.

9. Rational Emotive Behaviour Therapy (REBT):

- **Dispute Irrational Beliefs:** Use REBT techniques to identify and dispute irrational beliefs contributing to negative thoughts.
- **Replace Irrational Thoughts:** Replace irrational thoughts with more rational and adaptive beliefs.

10. Set Realistic Goals:

- **Break Down Goals:** Instead of setting overwhelming goals, break them down into smaller, more manageable steps.
- **Celebrate Achievements:** Acknowledge and celebrate your achievements, no matter how small, to reinforce a positive mindset.

11. Professional Support:

- **Therapy:** Consider seeking the help of a mental health professional, such as a cognitive-behavioural therapist, who can guide you through techniques tailored to your specific challenges.

12. Mind-Body Techniques:

- **Deep Breathing:** Practice deep breathing exercises to calm the mind and reduce the emotional intensity of negative thoughts.
- **Progressive Muscle Relaxation (PMR):** Learn PMR techniques to release physical tension associated with negative thinking.

Building a supportive network is crucial for mental and emotional well-being. A strong support system can provide encouragement, understanding, and practical assistance during both challenging and positive times. Here are steps to help you build and strengthen a supportive network:

1. Identify Your Needs:

- Reflect on your emotional, practical, and social needs. Consider the type of support you require, whether it's emotional understanding, advice, or assistance with tasks.

2. Assess Existing Relationships:

- Identify people in your life who already offer support. This could include friends, family members, colleagues, or neighbours.

3. Cultivate Existing Relationships:

- Strengthen bonds with people you already know and trust. Communicate openly, share your thoughts and feelings, and express your needs.

4. Expand Your Social Circle:

- Join clubs, classes, or groups related to your interests. This provides opportunities to meet new people who share your passions.

5. Be Open and Approachable:

- Foster an open and approachable demeanour. Make an effort to connect with others and be willing to share your experiences.

6. Reciprocity:

- Build relationships based on mutual support. Be willing to give as much as you receive, creating a reciprocal and balanced dynamic.

7. Join Supportive Communities:

- Participate in online or local communities focused on areas of interest, personal development, or shared experiences. This can create a sense of belonging.

8. Communicate Effectively:

- Practice clear and effective communication. Express your needs, boundaries, and feelings openly. Listen actively to others.

9. Encourage Positivity:

- Surround yourself with positive influences. Seek relationships that uplift and inspire you.

10. Participate in Group Activities:

- Engage in group activities or events where you can connect with others who share similar interests or goals.

11. Volunteer:

- Offer your time and skills to volunteer for causes you care about. This not only provides a sense of purpose but also connects you with like-minded individuals.

12. Attend Networking Events:

- Attend events in your community or industry to expand your professional network. Networking can lead to valuable connections and support.

13. Utilize Technology:

- Stay connected through social media, messaging apps, and video calls. Virtual connections can be just as meaningful as in-person ones.

14. Seek Professional Support:

- Consider therapy or counselling to receive professional support. Mental health professionals can offer guidance and tools for building a healthy support system.

15. Be Patient:

- Building a supportive network takes time. Be patient and allow relationships to develop naturally.

16. Join Support Groups:

- If you're dealing with specific challenges, consider joining support groups. These groups provide a space to share experiences and receive empathy.

17. Express Gratitude:

- Acknowledge and express gratitude for the support you receive. Gratitude strengthens relationships and encourages continued mutual support.

18. Healthy Boundaries:

- Establish and maintain healthy boundaries in relationships. Clear boundaries contribute to a more balanced and respectful support system.

Remember that a supportive network is diverse, encompassing various types of relationships and connections. Building and maintaining these connections requires ongoing effort, but the benefits for your well-being are significant.

Connection and healthy relationships play a vital role in shaping our overall well-being and contribute significantly to our mental, emotional, and even physical health. Understanding the importance of connection and fostering healthy relationships can lead to a more fulfilling and enriched life. Here's why these aspects are crucial:

1. Emotional Support:

- **Validation and Empathy:** Healthy relationships provide a space for emotional validation and empathy. Feeling understood and supported during challenging times is essential for mental well-being.

2. Reduced Stress:

- **Coping Together:** Sharing life's burdens with others helps reduce stress. Healthy relationships provide a support system during difficult situations, making challenges more manageable.

3. Sense of Belonging:

- **Community and Belonging:** Connection fosters a sense of belonging. Feeling part of a community or having close relationships fulfils a basic human need for social connection and acceptance.

4. Improved Mental Health:

- **Reduced Loneliness:** Social isolation and loneliness can negatively impact mental health. Healthy relationships counteract these effects by providing companionship and emotional connection.

5. Enhanced Physical Health:

- **Longevity:** Studies suggest that individuals with strong social connections tend to live longer. Positive relationships contribute to better physical health and immune system function.

6. Self-Esteem and Self-Worth:

- **Positive Reflection:** Healthy relationships contribute to positive self-esteem. Being valued and respected by others reflects positively on one's self-worth.

7. Communication Skills:

- **Improved Communication:** Healthy relationships enhance communication skills. Open and honest communication fosters understanding, resolving conflicts, and building stronger connections.

8. Personal Growth:

- **Challenges and Feedback:** Healthy relationships provide opportunities for personal growth. Challenges and constructive feedback from others can contribute to self-improvement.

9. Shared Joy and Celebration:

- **Celebrating Achievements:** Positive relationships allow for the sharing of joys and celebrations. Having someone to share successes with enhances the experience.

10. Stress Buffering:

- **Support During Challenges:** During life's challenges, having a supportive network act as a buffer, helping individuals cope more effectively with stressors.

11. Resilience:

- **Crisis Support:** Healthy relationships contribute to resilience. Facing crises with a support system provides emotional strength and the ability to navigate difficulties.

12. Altruism and Compassion:

- **Acts of Kindness:** Healthy relationships often involve acts of kindness, compassion, and altruism. Engaging in these behaviours deepens connections and contributes to a positive social environment.

13. Interdependence:

- **Shared Resources:** Healthy relationships encourage interdependence, where individuals can rely on each other for mutual support and shared resources.

14. Moral and Ethical Support:

- **Guidance and Perspective:** Healthy relationships provide moral and ethical support. Trusted individuals can offer guidance and different perspectives, aiding in decision-making.

15. Happiness and Fulfilment:

- **Emotional Fulfilment:** Ultimately, healthy relationships contribute to a sense of happiness and fulfilment. Knowing that one is loved, understood, and supported adds significant value to life.

16. Improved Coping Skills:

- **Learning from Others:** Observing how others navigate challenges in healthy relationships provides valuable insights and improves one's own coping skills.

Understanding the significance of connection and cultivating healthy relationships involves intentional effort, effective communication, and mutual respect. Prioritizing these elements contributes to a more resilient, fulfilling, and satisfying life.

Navigating relationships successfully involves effective communication, mutual understanding, and seeking support when needed. Here are some key principles and strategies to help you navigate relationships and foster healthy communication with loved ones:

1. Open and Honest Communication:

- **Express Yourself Clearly:** Clearly communicate your thoughts, feelings, and needs. Be open and honest about your experiences and expectations
- **Active Listening:** Practice active listening by giving your full attention, making eye contact, and validating the other person's feelings.

2. Use "I" Statements:

- **Own Your Feelings:** Frame your expressions using "I" statements to take ownership of your feelings. For example, say "I feel" instead of "You always" to avoid sounding accusatory.

3. Avoid Assumptions:

- **Seek Clarification:** When in doubt, ask for clarification. Avoid making assumptions about the other person's thoughts or intentions.

4. Choose the Right Time and Place:

- **Timing Matters:** Select an appropriate time to discuss important matters Avoid addressing sensitive issues when either party is stressed, angry, o distracted.

5. Be Respectful:

- **Respect Differences:** Recognize and respect each other's differences. Celebrate diversity and appreciate that individuals may have unique perspectives.

6. Set Boundaries:

- **Establish Clear Boundaries:** Clearly define and communicate personal boundaries. Respect each other's limits and be willing to negotiate when necessary.

7. Show Empathy:

- **Put Yourself in Their Shoes:** Practice empathy by trying to understand the other person's perspective. Validate their feelings even if you don't agree.

8. Express Appreciation:

- **Show Gratitude:** Regularly express appreciation for the positive aspects of the relationship. Acknowledge efforts and contributions made by the other person.

9. Apologize and Forgive:

- **Take Responsibility:** If you make a mistake, apologize sincerely. Be willing to forgive when the other person apologizes.
- **Let Go of Grudges:** Holding onto resentment can strain relationships. Work towards letting go of grudges and moving forward.

10. Seek Support When Needed:

- **Share Your Feelings:** Don't hesitate to share your feelings and concerns with loved ones. Seeking emotional support is a healthy way to navigate challenges.
- **Professional Support:** If necessary, consider seeking guidance from a therapist or counselor to navigate more complex issues.

11. Practice Mindfulness:

- **Stay Present:** Be mindful during conversations. Avoid distractions and stay present to fully engage in the discussion.

12. Collaborative Problem-Solving:

- **Work Together:** Approach challenges as a team. Collaborate on finding solutions rather than viewing issues as a source of conflict.

13. Celebrate Achievements:

- **Share Successes:** Celebrate each other's achievements and milestones. Positive reinforcement strengthens the bond between individuals.

14. Cultivate Mutual Interests:

- **Find Common Ground:** Cultivate shared interests and activities. This creates opportunities for bonding and spending quality time together.

15. Be Patient and Understanding:

- **Practice Patience:** Relationships require time and effort. Be patient with each other's growth and development.

- **Understand Growth and Change:** Recognize that people evolve over time. Embrace growth and change as a natural part of life.

Effective communication and seeking support contribute to the resilience and strength of relationships. By fostering open and respectful dialogue, addressing challenges collaboratively, and acknowledging the importance of emotional support, individuals can navigate relationships successfully.

How to offer support for someone dealing with Depression.

Encouraging someone to seek professional help, including therapy and medication options, is a delicate but important conversation. Here are some tips on how to approach and encourage someone to explore these options:

1. Express Concern and Empathy:

- **Start with Care:** Begin the conversation by expressing genuine concern for their well-being. Use empathetic language to convey that you've noticed their struggles.

2. Use "I" Statements:

- **Avoid Accusations:** Frame your concern using "I" statements to avoid sounding accusatory. For example, say "I've noticed you've been struggling, and I'm concerned" instead of "You need help."

3. Highlight the Normalcy of Seeking Help:

- **Normalize Seeking Support:** Emphasize that seeking professional help is a common and positive step many people take to improve their mental health.

4. Share Personal Experiences:

- **Relatable Stories:** If you feel comfortable, share your own positive experiences with therapy or medication. This can help reduce stigma and show that seeking help is a sign of strength.

5. Provide Information:

- **Educate on Benefits:** Share information about the potential benefits of therapy and medication. Discuss how these options can provide coping strategies and support.

6. Highlight Professional Expertise:

- **Trained Professionals:** Emphasize that therapists and mental health professionals are trained to offer support and guidance. They can provide objective insights to help navigate challenges.

7. Offer to Assist:

- **Supportive Role:** Offer to assist in finding a suitable therapist or researching medication options. Your willingness to help can ease the process.

8. Acknowledge Concerns:

- **Address Fears and Concerns:** Acknowledge any fears or concerns they may have about therapy or medication. Addressing these reservations can help make the idea more approachable.

9. Highlight Empowerment:

- **Taking Control:** Encourage the idea that seeking help is a proactive step towards taking control of one's mental health. It can empower them to make positive changes.

10. Emphasize Confidentiality:

- **Privacy in Therapy:** Highlight the confidentiality of therapy sessions, assuring them that what is discussed is private and protected.

11. Collaborative Decision-Making:

- **Include Them in Decisions:** Encourage a collaborative approach by involving them in decisions about the type of help they seek and the professionals they choose.

12. Discuss Potential Benefits:

- **Improved Quality of Life:** Discuss how therapy and/or medication can contribute to an improved quality of life, better relationships, and enhanced overall well-being.

13. Provide Resources:

- **Share Resources:** Offer information about local mental health resources, hotlines, or websites where they can find more information about therapy and medication.

14. Be Patient and Non-Judgmental:

- **Respect Their Pace:** Recognize that the decision to seek professional help is personal. Be patient and non-judgmental, allowing them to proceed at their own pace.

15. Offer Ongoing Support:

- **Continued Support:** Reassure them that you will continue to offer support throughout the process. Your ongoing support can be a crucial factor in their journey.

Remember that every individual is different, and their response may vary. Encourage them to consult with a mental health professional to discuss their unique situation and explore the most suitable options for their needs.

Finding light in the darkness of depression can be a challenging journey, but it's crucial for healing and resilience. Here are some strategies that individuals experiencing depression might find helpful:

1. Reach Out for Support:

- **Connect with Others:** Share your feelings with trusted friends, family, or a mental health professional. Connection can provide comfort and understanding.

2. Professional Help:

- **Therapy and Counselling:** Seek the support of a therapist or counsellor. Professional guidance can help explore the root causes of depression and develop coping strategies.

3. Mindfulness and Meditation:

- **Present Moment Awareness:** Practice mindfulness and meditation to stay grounded in the present moment. Mindful breathing exercises can help manage overwhelming thoughts.

4. Creative Outlets:

- **Art, Writing, Music:** Engage in creative activities as a form of expression. Writing in a journal, creating art, or playing music can be therapeutic.

5. Establish a Routine:

- **Structure and Predictability:** Create a daily routine to provide structure and predictability. Small, achievable goals can help regain a sense of control.

6. Physical Exercise:

- **Mood-Boosting Activities:** Engage in regular physical exercise. Even a short walk can release endorphins, which are natural mood lifters.

7. Nature Connection:

- **Spending Time Outdoors:** Spend time in nature. Exposure to natural light and the outdoors has positive effects on mood.

8. Set Realistic Goals:

- **Break Down Tasks:** Set small, achievable goals. Celebrate even the smallest accomplishments to build a sense of achievement.

9. Practice Self-Compassion:

- **Be Kind to Yourself:** Treat yourself with kindness. Understand that struggling with depression doesn't reflect personal failure, and self-compassion is crucial.

0. Identify Triggers:

- **Understand Your Triggers:** Identify situations or activities that may trigger depressive feelings. Awareness allows for better preparation and coping.

1. Medication Evaluation:

- **Consult a psychiatrist:** If appropriate, consider consulting a psychiatrist to discuss medication options. Medication can be a valuable part of treatment for some individuals.

2. Cognitive Behavioural Therapy (CBT):

- **Challenge Negative Thoughts:** Explore cognitive-behavioural therapy to identify and challenge negative thought patterns contributing to depression.

3. Mind-Body Practices:

- **Yoga or Tai Chi:** Explore mind-body practices like yoga or tai chi. These activities combine physical movement with mindfulness.

4. Volunteer Work:

- **Purpose and Connection:** Engage in volunteer work to find purpose and connection. Helping others can have a positive impact on your own well-being.

5. Educate Yourself:

- **Understanding Depression:** Learn more about depression. Understanding the condition can empower you to make informed decisions about your well-being.

16. Celebrate Small Wins:

- **Acknowledge Progress:** Celebrate small victories. Acknowledge and appreciate any progress, no matter how incremental.

17. Establish a Support System:

- **Lean on Loved Ones:** Cultivate a support system. Share your journey with those who care about you and let them provide assistance and encouragement.

18. Embrace Hope:

- **Focus on the Future:** Cultivate a sense of hope. Remind yourself that depression is treatable, and with time and support, things can improve.

Remember that overcoming depression is a gradual process, and seeking professional help is a courageous step. Combining various strategies and customizing them to fit your unique needs can contribute to finding light in the darkness of depression. If you or someone you know is struggling with depression, reaching out to a mental health professional is essential for personalized support and guidance.

Unleashing creativity through artistic expression can be a powerful and therapeutic way to explore emotions, reduce stress, and promote overall well-being. Here are ways to discover the therapeutic power of artistic expression:

1. Explore Different Art Forms:

- **Visual Arts:** Experiment with drawing, painting, or sculpting.
- **Writing:** Try journaling, poetry, or storytelling.
- **Performing Arts:** Explore music, dance, or theatre.

2. Create a Safe Space:

- **Designate a Creative Space:** Set up a dedicated space for your artistic endeavours. Make it a comfortable and safe environment where you can freely express yourself.

3. Mindful Art Practices:

- **Practice Mindfulness:** Engage in art mindfully, focusing on the process rather than the end result. This can promote relaxation and self-awareness.

4. Express Emotions:

- **Use Colours and Symbols:** Channel emotions into your artwork using colours, shapes, and symbols. Art can be a non-verbal way to express complex feelings.

5. Art Therapy:

- **Professional Guidance:** Consider art therapy with a trained art therapist. This form of therapy uses artistic expression to explore emotions and enhance mental health.

6. Art Journaling:

- **Combine Art and Writing:** Use an art journal to combine visual expression with written reflection. This allows for a holistic exploration of thoughts and emotions.

7. Collaborative Art:

- **Join Group Projects:** Collaborate with others on art projects. This fosters a sense of community and shared creativity.

8. Music for Relaxation:

- **Listen and Create:** Listen to calming music or create your own tunes. Music can be a powerful tool for emotional expression and stress relief.

9. Movement and Dance:

- **Express through Movement:** Dance freely to express emotions and release tension. Movement can be a form of embodied artistic expression.

10. Photography and Nature:

- **Capture Moments:** Use photography to document moments and perspectives. Spending time in nature with a camera can be both therapeutic and creative.

11. Experiment with Different Materials:

- **Mixed Media:** Combine various materials and textures in your artwork. Experimenting with different mediums can enhance creativity.

12. Art as a Form of Meditation:

- **Focus on the Process:** Engage in art as a form of meditation. Allow the repetitive nature of creating to calm the mind and promote a meditative state.

13. Art Classes or Workshops:

- **Structured Learning:** Take art classes or workshops to learn new techniques and connect with a community of fellow artists.

14. Transform Challenges into Art:

- **Art as Catharsis:** Use art to process challenges or difficult experiences. Creating can serve as a form of catharsis and healing.

15. Create a Visual Manifestation:

- **Vision Boards:** Develop a vision board to visually represent your goals, dreams, and aspirations. This can provide a daily source of inspiration.

16. Art Exhibitions or Showcasing:

- **Share Your Creations:** Consider showcasing your art, whether in exhibitions, online platforms, or among friends. Sharing can foster a sense of accomplishment.

17. Art Retreats:

- **Immersive Experiences:** Attend art retreats or immersive creative experiences to deepen your connection with artistic expression.

18. Celebrate Imperfections:

- **Embrace the Process:** Allow imperfections in your creations. Embracing the process, including mistakes, can be a powerful lesson in self-acceptance.

Remember, the goal is not perfection but personal expression and self-discovery. Whether you're an experienced artist or just starting, the therapeutic benefits of artistic expression are accessible to everyone. Engaging in creative activities regularly can contribute to a greater sense of well-being and joy in life.

The healing embrace of nature and harnessing the transformative energy of the natural world can have profound positive effects on mental, emotional, and physical well-being. Here are ways to embrace nature for healing and transformation:

1. Forest Bathing (Shinrin-Yoku):

- **Immerse Yourself in Nature:** Spend time in a forest or natural environment, immersing yourself in the sights, sounds, and smells. Forest bathing has been shown to reduce stress and improve mood.

2. Grounding Practices:

- **Connect with the Earth:** Practice grounding by walking barefoot on natural surfaces like grass, sand, or soil. This can enhance a sense of connection with the Earth.

3. Nature Walks:

- **Mindful Walking:** Take mindful walks in nature. Pay attention to the sensations of each step and observe the natural surroundings without distraction.

4. Outdoor Meditation:

- **Meditate in Nature:** Find a peaceful spot in nature for meditation. Use the sounds of birds, rustling leaves, or flowing water as points of focus.

5. Water Therapy:

- **Be by Water:** Spend time near water, whether it's a river, lake, or ocean. The calming sound of water has therapeutic effects on the mind.

6. Nature Journaling:

- **Reflect on Nature:** Keep a nature journal to document your observations, feelings, and experiences while spending time outdoors.

7. Sunlight Exposure:

- **Get Sunlight:** Exposure to natural sunlight helps regulate circadian rhythms and boosts mood. Spend time outdoors during daylight hours.

8. Nature Retreats:

- **Immersive Experiences:** Consider attending nature retreats or wellness programs set in natural surroundings for a deeper connection and transformation.

9. Nature Art and Creativity:

- **Express Through Art:** Use natural materials to create art. This can be a therapeutic way to express creativity and connect with the environment.

10. Nature Photography:

- **Capture Beauty:** Explore photography in nature. Capturing the beauty around you can enhance mindfulness and appreciation.

11. Camping and Stargazing:

- **Under the Stars:** Spend a night camping and stargazing. Being under the open sky fosters a sense of awe and wonder.

12. Botanical Gardens or Arboretums:

- **Explore Green Spaces:** Visit botanical gardens or arboretums to surround yourself with diverse plant life and experience the healing power of nature.

13. Outdoor Yoga:

- **Connect Body and Nature:** Practice yoga outdoors. Connect your movements with the natural environment to enhance the mind-body connection.

14. Nature Sounds for Relaxation:

- **Listen Mindfully:** Use recordings of nature sounds for relaxation. This can be especially beneficial for those who may not have immediate access to natural spaces.

15. Volunteer in Conservation:

- **Active Involvement:** Get involved in conservation projects or community gardening. Actively participating in the care of natural spaces can be transformative.

16. Nature-Based Mindfulness Practices:

- **Guided Nature Meditations:** Listen to guided nature meditations that take you on a mental journey through natural landscapes.

17. Therapeutic Gardens:

- **Engage with Healing Gardens:** Spend time in therapeutic gardens designed to promote relaxation and well-being.

18. Digital Detox in Nature:

- **Disconnect Regularly:** Practice digital detox by spending dedicated time in nature without electronic devices. Allow yourself to fully engage with the natural world.

19. Nature as a Symbol:

- **Metaphorical Reflections:** Use nature as a metaphor for personal growth and transformation. Reflect on the changing seasons, resilience of trees, or the flow of water as symbolic representations.

20. Nature-Based Rituals:

- **Create Personal Rituals:** Establish personal rituals in nature, such as sunrise or sunset reflections, to cultivate a sense of connection and mindfulness.

Embracing the healing embrace of nature involves a conscious effort to integrate natural elements into daily life. Whether through simple daily walks, immersive nature experiences, or creative expressions inspired by the outdoors, the transformative energy of the natural world has the potential to enhance well-being and foster personal growth.

Cultivating mindfulness and incorporating meditation practices into your daily life can contribute to a calm and present state of mind. Here are some mindfulness practices and meditation techniques to help you foster a sense of calm presence:

1. Mindful Breathing:

- **Focused Attention:** Sit comfortably and focus your attention on your breath. Inhale and exhale naturally, observing the sensations of each breath. If your mind wanders, gently bring it back to the breath.

2. Body Scan Meditation:

- **Progressive Relaxation:** Lie down or sit comfortably. Slowly scan your body from head to toe, paying attention to each part. Release any tension or tightness as you move through each area.

3. Loving-Kindness Meditation:

- **Cultivate Compassion:** Extend wishes of love and kindness to yourself, loved ones, and even to those you may find challenging. Repeat phrases like "May I (you/they) be happy, may I (you/they) be healthy."

4. Mindful Walking:

- **Conscious Movement:** Take a slow walk, paying attention to each step. Notice the sensations in your feet and legs. Feel the connection between your body and the ground.

5. Breath Awareness Meditation:

- **Observing the Breath:** Find a quiet space, sit comfortably, and bring your attention to the breath. Observe the inhalation and exhalation without trying to control it. Notice the natural rhythm.

6. Mindful Eating:

- **Savor Each Bite:** During meals, pay attention to the Flavours, textures, and smells of your food. Eat slowly and savour each bite. Be fully present with the act of eating.

7. Body Awareness Meditation:

- **Sensations and Presence:** Sit or lie down and bring your attention to different parts of your body. Notice any sensations without judgment, simply observing the present moment.

8. Zen or Mindfulness Bell Meditation:

- **Bell Awareness:** Set a timer or use a mindfulness bell app. When the bell rings, bring your attention to the present moment. Allow the sound to anchor you in the now.

9. Observing Thoughts Meditation:

- **Non-Judgmental Awareness:** Sit quietly and observe your thoughts. Rather than getting entangled in them, become an observer. Allow thoughts to come and go without judgment.

10. Morning Mindfulness Routine:

- **Start the Day Mindfully:** Begin your day with a few minutes of mindfulness. This can include mindful breathing, setting positive intentions, or simply being present before starting your activities.

11. Mindful Listening:

- **Fully Engage in Conversations:** Practice attentive listening during conversations. Give your full attention, avoid interrupting, and truly hear what the other person is saying.

12. Gratitude Meditation:

- **Focus on Gratitude:** Reflect on things you're grateful for. It could be people, experiences, or even simple everyday moments. Cultivating gratitude enhances a sense of presence.

13. Mindful Technology Use:

- **Conscious Screen Time:** Be mindful of your technology use. Take breaks practice digital detox, and use technology intentionally rather than habitually.

14. Nature Mindfulness:

- **Connect with Nature:** Spend time outdoors. Whether it's a walk in the park, gardening, or simply sitting in nature, connect with the natural environment mindfully.

15. Evening Reflection:

- **Review Your Day:** Before bed, reflect on your day with a sense of mindfulness. Acknowledge both positive and challenging moments without judgment.

16. Mindful Stretching or Yoga:

- **Conscious Movement:** Incorporate mindful stretching or yoga into your routine. Focus on each movement, the breath, and the sensations in your body.

17. Mindful Breathing with Affirmations:

- **Positive Affirmations:** Combine mindful breathing with positive affirmations. Inhale positivity, exhale tension. Repeat affirmations silently or aloud.

18. Mindful Work Breaks:

- **Pause and Breathe:** Take mindful breaks during work. Step away, close your eyes, and take a few conscious breaths to refresh your mind.

19. Rainbow Meditation:

- **Colour Visualization:** Visualize each colour of the rainbow, starting with red and moving through the spectrum. Associate each colour with positive qualities or intentions.

20. Compassion Meditation:

- **Self-Compassion Practice:** Cultivate self-compassion by acknowledging your challenges and sending yourself wishes of love and understanding.

Remember, mindfulness is a skill that develops over time with regular practice. Find what resonates with you and integrate these practices into your daily life to nurture a calm and present state of mind.

Cultivating resilience and hope is essential for navigating life's challenges and maintaining overall well-being. Resilience is the ability to bounce back from adversity, while hope provides the motivation to move forward with a positive outlook. Here are strategies to cultivate resilience and hope:

Cultivating Resilience:

- **Positive Self-Talk:**
  - o **Challenge Negative Thoughts:** Identify and challenge negative thoughts. Replace them with more positive and realistic affirmations.
- **Mindfulness and Acceptance:**
  - o **Present-Moment Awareness:** Practice mindfulness to stay grounded in the present moment. Accept what you cannot change and focus on what you can control.
- **Build Strong Connections:**
  - o **Social Support:** Cultivate supportive relationships with friends, family, or a community. Social connections provide a strong foundation for resilience.
- **Adaptability:**
  - o **Flexible Thinking:** Develop a flexible mindset. Be open to adapting your goals and strategies in response to changing circumstances.
- **Problem-Solving Skills:**
  - o **Break Challenges into Steps:** Break down challenges into smaller, manageable steps. Develop problem-solving skills to tackle each step effectively.
- **Optimism and Positivity:**
  - o **Focus on the Positive:** Cultivate an optimistic outlook. Acknowledge positive aspects of situations, even in the face of difficulties.
- **Self-Compassion:**
  - o **Be Kind to Yourself:** Treat yourself with kindness and understanding. Acknowledge that setbacks are a natural part of life.
- **Learn from Adversity:**
  - o **Growth Mindset:** View challenges as opportunities for growth. Learn from difficult experiences and use them to build resilience.
- **Physical Well-Being:**
  - o **Healthy Lifestyle:** Prioritize physical health through regular exercise, balanced nutrition, and sufficient sleep. Physical well-being supports emotional resilience.
- **Seek Professional Support:**
  - o **Therapy or Counselling:** If needed, seek the guidance of a mental health professional. Therapy can provide tools and strategies to enhance resilience.

Cultivating Hope:

- **Set Realistic Goals:**

- o **Small Achievable Steps:** Set realistic and achievable goals. Breaking down larger goals into smaller steps makes them more manageable.
- **Visualize Success:**
  - o **Positive Imagery:** Visualize a positive outcome for your goals. Create mental images of success to reinforce hope and motivation.
- **Maintain a Positive Focus:**
  - o **Gratitude Practice:** Cultivate a gratitude practice. Regularly reflect on and express gratitude for positive aspects of your life.
- **Celebrate Progress:**
  - o **Acknowledge Achievements:** Celebrate even small victories. Acknowledging progress reinforces a sense of accomplishment and fuels hope.
- **Surround Yourself with Positivity:**
  - o **Supportive Environment:** Surround yourself with positive influences, whether it's people, media, or environments that uplift and inspire.
- **Learn from Setbacks:**
  - o **Resilience in Setbacks:** View setbacks as temporary and as opportunities to learn and grow. Resilience and hope often go hand in hand.
- **Create a Vision Board:**
  - o **Visual Representation:** Make a vision board that represents your hopes and aspirations. Visual reminders can inspire and reinforce positive feelings.
- **Connect with Inspirational Stories:**
  - o **Role Models:** Learn about people who have overcome adversity. Their stories can provide inspiration and reinforce the possibility of positive outcomes.
- **Stay Engaged in Activities:**
  - o **Pursue Passions:** Engage in activities that bring you joy and fulfilment. Pursuing passions adds purpose and enhances hope.
- **Encourage a Positive Inner Dialogue:**
  - o **Positive Self-Talk:** Develop a positive inner dialogue. Challenge negative thoughts and replace them with hopeful and encouraging affirmations.
- **Mindful Reflection:**
  - o **Reflect on Progress:** Periodically reflect on the progress you've made. Acknowledge the steps you've taken toward your goals.
- **Connect with a Supportive Community:**
  - o **Share Hopes and Goals:** Connect with a community that supports your aspirations. Sharing your hopes with others creates a sense of shared vision.
- **Stay Curious and Open-Minded:**

- o **Explore Possibilities:** Cultivate curiosity and open-mindedness. Stay open to new possibilities and be curious about the potential for positive change.
- **Contribute to Others:**
  - o **Acts of Kindness:** Engage in acts of kindness and contribute to others. Altruistic actions can foster a sense of purpose and hope.

Cultivating resilience and hope is an ongoing process that involves intentional practices and a positive mindset. By incorporating these strategies into your daily life, you can enhance your ability to navigate challenges, bounce back from adversity, and maintain a hopeful outlook for the future.

Shifting perspective and finding gratitude in the darkest moments can be a powerful practice that fosters resilience and emotional well-being. Here are some strategies to help shift your perspective and cultivate gratitude even when facing challenging circumstances:

- **Acknowledge Your Feelings:** Start by recognizing and accepting your emotions. It's okay to feel upset, frustrated, or disappointed in challenging situations. Acknowledging your feelings is the first step towards understanding them.
- **Practice Mindfulness:** Engage in mindfulness techniques to stay present and focused. Meditation, deep breathing, or simply paying attention to your surroundings can help shift your perspective from the challenges to the current moment, allowing you to find gratitude in small things.
- **Keep a Gratitude Journal:** Regularly write down things you are grateful for, even in difficult times. This can be a powerful tool to remind yourself of the positive aspects of your life. Reflect on both big and small blessings.
- **Seek Silver Linings:** Train your mind to find the silver linings in challenging situations. Ask yourself what you can learn from the experience or how it might contribute to personal growth. This shift in focus can foster a sense of gratitude.
- **Connect with Supportive People:** Surround yourself with positive and supportive individuals. Sharing your feelings with others can provide new perspectives and insights. It can also remind you of the positive aspects of your relationships.
- **Set Realistic Expectations:** Adjust your expectations to be more realistic, especially during challenging times. Understand that life has its ups and downs, and not every moment will be perfect. Adjusting your expectations can make it easier to find gratitude in imperfect situations.
- **Practice Self-Compassion:** Be kind to yourself during tough times. Treat yourself with the same compassion you would offer a friend facing similar

challenges. Acknowledge your efforts and give yourself credit for navigating difficulties.
- **Focus on What You Can Control:** Identify aspects of the situation that you can control and take action where possible. Shifting your focus to what you can influence empowers you and helps cultivate a sense of gratitude for your ability to make positive changes.
- **Celebrate Small Wins:** Recognize and celebrate even the smallest victories. Whether it's overcoming a minor obstacle or achieving a small goal, acknowledging these accomplishments can help shift your perspective towards gratitude.
- **Volunteer or Help Others:** Engaging in acts of kindness or volunteering can provide a sense of purpose and perspective. Helping others who may be facing challenges can highlight the positive impact you can have, fostering gratitude.

Remember, cultivating gratitude is a gradual process, and it's okay to take small steps. Consistent practice of these strategies can contribute to a more positive mindset, even in the face of challenging circumstances.

Building inner strength and resilience is crucial for bouncing back from adversity. Here are some strategies to help you cultivate inner strength:

- **Cultivate a Growth Mindset:** Embrace challenges as opportunities for growth rather than insurmountable obstacles. View setbacks as a chance to learn and improve, fostering resilience in the face of adversity.
- **Develop Self-Awareness:** Understand your strengths and weaknesses. Knowing yourself well enables you to navigate challenges more effectively and build upon your strengths during difficult times.
- **Build a Support System:** Cultivate relationships with friends, family, or a support network. Having a strong support system provides emotional reinforcement and practical assistance during tough times.
- **Practice Self-Compassion:** Be kind to yourself. Acknowledge that everyone faces challenges, and it's okay not to be perfect. Treat yourself with the same kindness and understanding you would offer a friend.
- **Set Realistic Goals:** Break down larger goals into smaller, more achievable steps. Celebrate small victories along the way, reinforcing your ability to overcome challenges.
- **Foster Adaptability:** Develop the ability to adapt to change. Life is often unpredictable, and being flexible in the face of adversity can help you navigate challenges more effectively.
- **Maintain a Positive Perspective:** Look for the silver lining in difficult situations. Focus on what you can control and work towards positive outcomes. Optimism can be a powerful tool for building inner strength.

- **Learn from Adversity:** Reflect on past challenges and consider what you've learned from them. Use this knowledge to build resilience and develop coping mechanisms for future difficulties.
- **Practice Mindfulness and Stress Reduction:** Incorporate mindfulness techniques into your daily routine to stay present and manage stress. Techniques such as meditation, deep breathing, or yoga can promote emotional well-being.
- **Develop Problem-Solving Skills:** Instead of feeling overwhelmed by challenges, break them down into manageable parts and develop effective problem-solving strategies. Focus on finding solutions rather than dwelling on the problems.
- **Maintain Physical Health:** Regular exercise, a balanced diet, and sufficient sleep contribute to physical and mental well-being. Taking care of your body enhances your ability to face challenges with resilience.
- **Engage in Activities You Enjoy:** Pursue hobbies and activities that bring you joy and a sense of accomplishment. Engaging in enjoyable activities can provide a mental and emotional boost during difficult times.
- **Seek Professional Help if Needed:** If you find it challenging to bounce back from adversity on your own, consider seeking support from a mental health professional. They can provide guidance and tools to build resilience.

Remember that building inner strength is an ongoing process, and it's okay to seek help when needed. By incorporating these strategies into your life, you can develop the resilience to bounce back from adversity with greater strength and confidence.

Embracing hope and nurturing the belief in a brighter future and a life beyond depression

Embracing hope and nurturing the belief in a brighter future is crucial for individuals facing depression. Here are some strategies to foster hope and cultivate a positive outlook:

Set Realistic Goals: Break down larger goals into smaller, achievable steps. Setting and accomplishing realistic goals can provide a sense of purpose and achievement, contributing to a more positive outlook.

Create a Vision for the Future: Envision the kind of life you want to lead beyond depression. What activities bring you joy? What relationships do you want to nurture? Creating a positive vision for the future can inspire hope and motivation.

Surround Yourself with Support: Build a strong support network of friends, family, or mental health professionals. Sharing your feelings with others and receiving support can provide a sense of connection and reinforce the belief that you are not alone in your journey.

Practice Self-Compassion: Be kind to yourself and acknowledge that overcoming depression is a process. Treat yourself with the same compassion you would offer a friend. Avoid self-criticism and focus on self-care.

Seek Professional Help: Reach out to mental health professionals who can provide guidance and support. Therapy, counselling, or medication may be part of your treatment plan. A mental health professional can help you develop coping strategies and work towards a brighter future.

Engage in Activities You Enjoy: Identify activities that bring you pleasure or a sense of accomplishment. Whether it's a hobby, exercise, or creative pursuits, engaging in activities you enjoy can contribute to a more positive mindset.

Mindfulness and Meditation: Practice mindfulness and meditation to stay present and manage negative thoughts. These practices can help you develop a greater awareness of your thoughts and feelings, allowing you to respond more positively to challenges.

Educate Yourself about Depression: Understanding depression and its treatment options can empower you in your journey. Knowledge about the condition can reduce feelings of helplessness and encourage proactive steps towards recovery.

Celebrate Progress, No Matter How Small: Acknowledge and celebrate even the smallest steps forward. Recognizing progress, no matter how incremental, reinforces the belief that positive change is possible.

Create a Daily Routine: Establishing a routine provides structure and stability. Incorporate activities that promote well-being, such as regular exercise, proper nutrition, and sufficient sleep.

Challenge Negative Thoughts: Learn to recognize and challenge negative thoughts. Cognitive-behavioural therapy (CBT) is a therapeutic approach that can help you identify and reframe negative thought patterns.

Explore New Possibilities: Be open to exploring new interests, friendships, or career paths. Embracing change and new possibilities can create a sense of hope and excitement for the future.

Express Gratitude: Take time each day to reflect on things you are grateful for. This practice can shift your focus towards positive aspects of your life, fostering a sense of hope and appreciation.

Remember that recovery from depression is a gradual process, and everyone's journey is unique. Embracing hope involves taking small steps each day and being patient with yourself as you work towards a brighter and more fulfilling future. If you're struggling, don't hesitate to seek professional help.

"Thriving in the light" can be interpreted in various ways, encompassing personal growth, positivity, and a flourishing life. Here are some suggestions to capture the essence of thriving in the light:

- **Cultivate a Positive Mindset:** Train your mind to focus on the positive aspects of life. Practice gratitude and look for the bright side in challenging situations. A positive mindset can significantly impact your overall well-being.
- **Embrace Growth and Learning:** View challenges as opportunities for growth. Continuously seek to learn and expand your skills. Embracing a mindset of lifelong learning contributes to personal development and success.
- **Surround Yourself with Positivity:** Choose to be around people who uplift and inspire you. Positive relationships can have a profound impact on your mood and outlook. Create a supportive network that encourages your growth and well-being.
- **Set and Pursue Meaningful Goals:** Define your goals and aspirations, aligning them with your values. Working towards objectives that have personal significance can bring a sense of purpose and fulfilment.
- **Prioritize Self-Care:** Take care of your physical, emotional, and mental well-being. Make self-care a priority by getting enough rest, engaging in activities you enjoy, and maintaining a healthy lifestyle.
- **Connect with Nature:** Spend time in nature to rejuvenate your spirit. Whether it's a walk in the park, hiking, or simply enjoying the outdoors, connecting with nature can have a positive impact on your mood and overall well-being.
- **Practice Mindfulness:** Incorporate mindfulness practices into your daily routine. This can include meditation, deep breathing exercises, or simply being fully present in the moment. Mindfulness can enhance your awareness and appreciation of life.
- **Celebrate Achievements:** Acknowledge and celebrate your accomplishments, no matter how small. Recognizing your successes reinforces a positive self-image and motivates you to continue thriving.

- **Cultivate Resilience:** Develop resilience to bounce back from challenges. Understand that setbacks are a natural part of life, and your ability to adapt and persevere contributes to your overall sense of thriving.
- **Express Creativity:** Engage in creative activities that bring you joy. Whether it's art, music, writing, or any other form of expression, tapping into your creativity can enhance your sense of fulfilment.
- **Foster Positive Habits:** Build positive habits that contribute to your well-being. This could include regular exercise, healthy eating, adequate sleep, and other habits that support a thriving lifestyle.
- **Cultivate Gratitude Daily:** Practice gratitude regularly by reflecting on the positive aspects of your life. This can be done through journaling or simply taking a moment each day to express gratitude for the blessings in your life.

Remember, thriving is a personal journey, and what brings light and fulfilment to one person may differ from another. Tailor these suggestions to align with your values and aspirations, creating a path that allows you to thrive in your unique way.

Embracing a new chapter and charting a path towards long-term recovery is a courageous and empowering journey. Here are some strategies to help you navigate this transformative process:

- **Set Clear and Achievable Goals:** Define specific, realistic, and achievable goals for your recovery. Break them down into smaller steps, making the journey more manageable and providing a sense of accomplishment along the way.
- **Develop a Comprehensive Recovery Plan:** Work with healthcare professionals to create a comprehensive recovery plan. This may include medical treatment, therapy, support groups, and lifestyle changes. Having a structured plan can provide guidance and a roadmap for your journey.
- **Build a Supportive Network:** Surround yourself with a supportive network of friends, family, and healthcare professionals. Establishing a strong support system is crucial for encouragement, understanding, and assistance during challenging times.
- **Cultivate Self-Compassion:** Be kind to yourself throughout the recovery process. Acknowledge that setbacks may occur and treat yourself with the same compassion and understanding that you would offer to a friend facing similar challenges.
- **Engage in Therapy and Counselling:** Regularly attend therapy or counselling sessions to address the psychological aspects of your recovery. Therapists can provide guidance, tools, and a safe space for exploration and healing.

- **Implement Healthy Lifestyle Changes:** Integrate positive lifestyle changes, such as regular exercise, a balanced diet, and sufficient sleep. These habits contribute to overall well-being and support the recovery process.
- **Establish Routine and Structure:** Create a daily routine to provide structure and stability. A consistent routine can be grounding and help you stay focused on your recovery goals.
- **Celebrate Milestones:** Acknowledge and celebrate the milestones in your recovery journey. Whether big or small, these achievements signify progress and serve as a source of motivation.
- **Mindfulness and Stress Management:** Incorporate mindfulness techniques and stress management practices into your daily life. Techniques such as meditation and deep breathing can help you stay present and manage stress effectively.
- **Explore New Hobbies and Interests:** Engage in activities that bring you joy and fulfilment. Exploring new hobbies or rediscovering old interests can provide a sense of purpose and contribute to your overall well-being.
- **Address Underlying Issues:** Work with your healthcare team to identify and address any underlying issues contributing to your challenges. This may involve exploring trauma, unresolved emotions, or other factors that impact your well-being.
- **Educate Yourself About Your Condition:** Gain a thorough understanding of your condition and the recovery process. Knowledge empowers you to actively participate in your recovery and make informed decisions about your well-being.
- **Practice Patience and Persistence:** Recovery is a gradual process that requires patience and persistence. Understand that setbacks are a normal part of the journey. Stay committed to the long-term goal of sustained recovery.

Remember, the path to long-term recovery is unique to each individual. Be open to adapting these strategies to fit your needs, your circumstances and seek professional guidance when necessary. Embracing this new chapter is a courageous step towards a healthier and more fulfilling life.

Creating a holistic lifestyle that incorporates healthy habits into your daily routine involves addressing various aspects of your well-being, including physical, mental, emotional, and social dimensions. Here's a comprehensive guide to help you cultivate a holistic and healthy lifestyle:

- **Establish a Consistent Sleep Routine:** Prioritize quality sleep by establishing a regular sleep schedule. Aim for 7-9 hours of sleep per night, create a relaxing bedtime routine, and ensure your sleep environment is conducive to rest.

Nutrient-Rich Diet: Focus on a balanced and nutritious diet that includes a variety of fruits, vegetables, whole grains, lean proteins, and healthy fats. Stay hydrated by drinking an adequate amount of water throughout the day.

Regular Physical Activity: Incorporate regular exercise into your routine. Find activities you enjoy, whether it's walking, jogging, yoga, or dancing. Aim for at least 150 minutes of moderate-intensity exercise per week.

Mindful Eating: Practice mindful eating by paying attention to your body's hunger and fullness cues. Avoid distractions while eating and savour the flavours and textures of your food.

Stress Management Techniques: Learn and practice stress management techniques such as deep breathing, meditation, or mindfulness. These practices can help reduce stress and promote a sense of calm.

Stay Hydrated: Drink an adequate amount of water throughout the day. Hydration is essential for overall health and well-being.

Cultivate Healthy Relationships: Nurture positive relationships with friends, family, and community. Social connections contribute to emotional well-being and provide support during challenging times.

Set Boundaries: Establish healthy boundaries in your personal and professional life. Learn to say no when necessary and prioritize activities that align with your values and goals.

Practice Gratitude: Cultivate a mindset of gratitude by regularly reflecting on and appreciating the positive aspects of your life. Keeping a gratitude journal can be a helpful practice.

Engage in Regular Self-Care: Dedicate time to self-care activities that bring you joy and relaxation. This could include reading, taking a bath, practicing a hobby, or spending time in nature.

Continuous Learning and Personal Growth: Foster a mindset of continuous learning and personal growth. Set aside time for reading, taking courses, or acquiring new skills that align with your interests and aspirations.

Limit Screen Time: Be mindful of your screen time, especially on electronic devices. Take breaks, practice the 20-20-20 rule (every 20 minutes, look at something 20 feet away for at least 20 seconds), and establish screen-free periods.

Regular Health Checkups: Schedule regular checkups and screenings to monitor your physical health. Attend dental and eye appointments and consult with healthcare professionals as needed.

Create a Relaxing Environment: Design your living space to promote relaxation and tranquillity. Consider incorporating elements such as plants, soft lighting, and comfortable furnishings.

Reflect and Set Intentions: Take time for self-reflection and set intentions for personal growth. Regularly assess your goals and make adjustments as needed to align with your evolving values and priorities.

Remember, creating a holistic lifestyle is a gradual process, and it's essential to tailor these habits to suit your individual needs and preferences. Consistency and small, sustainable changes over time can lead to significant improvements in your overall well-being.

- **Sarah's Journey to Recovery:** Sarah struggled with depression throughout her college years. She faced challenges with academic pressure, social anxiety, and feelings of inadequacy. Sarah decided to seek professional help and began therapy. Through consistent sessions, she explored the roots of her depression, developed coping mechanisms, and learned to challenge negative thought patterns.
- Sarah also embraced lifestyle changes, incorporating regular exercise, a balanced diet, and improved sleep habits. She gradually reconnected with friends and family, building a strong support system. Over time, Sarah regained a sense of purpose by setting small, achievable goals and celebrating her progress. Today, Sarah manages her mental health proactively, recognizing that ongoing self-care is crucial for maintaining her well-being.
- **James's Path to Resilience:** James experienced a major life setback that triggered a deep episode of depression. He faced challenges in his personal and professional life, leading to feelings of hopelessness. James reached out to both a therapist and a psychiatrist for support. With their guidance, he developed a treatment plan that included therapy, medication, and support groups.
- James learned to identify and challenge his negative thoughts, gradually shifting his perspective toward more positive thinking. He joined a local support group where he found understanding and connection with others facing similar struggles. James also prioritized physical health, incorporating regular exercise and a balanced diet into his routine. As he gained confidence and resilience, James transitioned back into work and began rebuilding his life. Today, he shares his experience to inspire others and reduce the stigma surrounding mental health.

Conclusion: A New Dawn

As we reach the final pages of "Embracing the Light," I invite you to reflect on the transformative journey we've undertaken together. This book has been a guide through the shadows, offering insights, strategies, and stories to inspire your personal evolution

Remember, the path to embracing the light is not always linear. It's a journey of twists and turns, peaks and valleys. Each chapter of your life contributes to the narrative, shaping your resilience, strength, and wisdom.

As you stand on the threshold of a new dawn, consider the lessons learned from those who have faced adversity and emerged stronger. Their stories echo the universal truth that, even in our darkest moments, the potential for growth and renewal exists.

Key Takeaways for Your Journey:

- **Resilience:** Embrace the challenges as opportunities for growth. Life's difficulties are not roadblocks but stepping stones towards your becoming.
- **Self-Compassion:** Extend the same kindness to yourself that you offer to others. In moments of struggle, remember that you are deserving of love and understanding.
- **Connection:** Cultivate meaningful connections with those who uplift and support you. Your network is a source of strength during both sunny days and storms.
- **Mindfulness:** Ground yourself in the present moment. Mindfulness is a lantern that guides you through the darkness, helping you find beauty even in the most unexpected places.
- **Purpose:** Discover or reaffirm your sense of purpose. What brings joy to your heart? What ignites your passion? These are the beacons leading you towards a more fulfilling life.
- **Continuous Growth:** Life is a continuous journey of growth. Embrace change, celebrate your progress, and remain open to the lessons yet to unfold.

As you close this chapter and embark on the next, know that the light within you is resilient, and it has the power to illuminate even the darkest corners of your soul. May your days ahead be filled with self-discovery, joy, and the warmth of your own inner light.

Wishing you a life embraced by the light,

Becca